TRUTH BE TOLD

New & Collected Premortems

Also by Thomas Farber

Fiction

The Beholder
A Lover's Question
Learning to Love It
Curves of Pursuit
Hazards to the Human Heart
Who Wrote the Book of Love?

Nonfiction

A Lover's Quarrel
Other Oceans (with Wayne Levin)
Provocations (with Robert Kuszek)
The Face of the Deep
Through a Liquid Mirror (with Wayne Levin)
On Water
Compared to What?
Too Soon to Tell
Rag Theatre (with Nacio Brown)
Tales for the Son of My Unborn Child

TRUTH BE TOLD

New & Collected Premortems

Thomas Farber

Hip Pocket Press
Managing Editor: Charles Entrekin
Nevada City, California
2005

Hip Pocket Press
228 Commercial St. #138
Nevada City, CA 95959

www.hippocketpress.com

Library of Congress Cataloging-in-Publication Data

Farber, Thomas, 1944 –
Truth be told: new & collected premortems / Thomas Farber.
v. cm.

ISBN 0-917658-33-7 (pbk. : alk. paper)

    I. Epigrams, American. 2. Epigrams — Authorship.
    I. Title. PS3556.A64T78 2005
    811'.54 — dc22   2005003927

For Isaías, *el noble analfabeto*

Acknowledgements

My thanks to Donald S. Ellis, who published the chapbook *The Price of the Ride*; to Peter Howard, who published the chapbook *Compressions: A Second Helping*; and to Oggetti Design for aesthetic guidance.

T.F.

Production: Mark Ostrov
Cover design: Brook Design Group

Contents

11

Introduction

The truth will out. In 1993, completing my first book of nonfiction about the Pacific, I was abducted by seventeenth century writer Francois (Duc de) La Rochefoucauld. Brutally subjected to his Maxims, I then found myself . . . trying some of my own. What ensued was a decade of reading and composing, presented here in *The Price of the Ride* (1996); *Compressions: A Second Helping* (1998); and the recently completed *Tongue-Tied: A Breviary of Cautions & Savors*. Also here are the companion essays for each, together comprising an appraisal of my fascination with this intensely self-conscious, often intemperate form.

Over the last ten years, among other projects, I wrote a second book of nonfiction about warm ocean and the Pacific, collaborated twice with marine photographer Wayne Levin, dreamed and completed a novel, and launched myself into a book on salsa — dance and music. If the epigrammatic never was all I was up to with language, neither was it far from my mind. I'd read aphorists; suddenly hear an idiom as if for the first time; tease out component energies of vices, virtues. Precise the genesis of this gag reflex, that. Would once more go to my late mother's dictionary to ascertain root, vector. I treasured revelations provoked by unexpected similarities, by rejuvenating word inversions, seemingly capricious juxtapositions, willfully mixed metaphors.

Here, as often as not, to connect the dots — to unpack meaning — the reader would have to be alert, rethink or reread a line that had initially required only an instant. Further, both form and content were frequently polemical (from the Greek, *polemos*, war). Disputatious, controverting. Contentious, not just in response to human foible or fate but because, in this medium with pretensions to the magisterially impersonal universal, the genially or implacably authoritative, the writer was willy-nilly exposing himself.

There's a Simon & Garfunkel line, "Hello darkness my old friend." Sometimes to again start writing is to salute the strangely familiar unknown, where one will have to blindly feel his way. There's a seductive eros in this recurrence, despite the sensation of risk: in darkness you can lead yourself astray. Among prose forms, the epigrammatic in particular gives ample opportunity to do just that, despite or while inducing the shock of recognition, the often perverse delight of illumination.

Now, surveying the mayhems presented here with the clarity of looking back, I confess to having savored partiality and the partial more than I should have. Accordingly, allow me to take this opportunity to retract each and every word.

T. F.
Berkeley, 2005

I

THE PRICE OF THE RIDE

A man in middle age sitting in an outdoor café. Two young women passing his table, walking faster than he thinks he'd be able to run after them.

Ⓧ

Turning fifty. Avoiding one's older friends. Lest what's happened to them prove contagious.

The vanity of self-loathing. He could be deemed a monster, but only by himself.

Sex: what puts you in contact with people you might otherwise never know.

He took the path of least regret.

＊

Loss of will. And, also, loss of won't.

＊

Sir Isaac Newton's gravity: what anyone of a certain age could have explained to him.

ꝗ

"Referred pain": inappropriate to a particular location, that is to say.

"I love you," she told him. And then, seeing his expression, added, laughing, "But don't worry, I'm very good at unrequited love."

❦

Recently separated. In bed with her lover, she says, "I do things for you I never did for my husband."

❦

Hair on torso, foliating, thickening. And just when he'd begun to feel really deciduous.

𝒳

Approaching the end: when a friend thinks of making you both executor and beneficiary of his estate. And, moved to tears, tells you. A kind of trading on the futures exchange.

Fastidious at fifty-five: no inconvenience too small to be avoided.

⟡

Not selfish, he was making the world safer for people like himself.

⟡

The complex, surprising lives of others. Envy as failure of the imagination.

⚜

False modesty: the writer who, enraged that Toni Morrison's won a Nobel Prize, is unable to come up with the name of someone he'd prefer.

⚜

Material times: the going rate of self-interest.

᠖

Said the rich womanizer, "The only things men fight over are sex and money."

᠖

To harden one's heart — against God, they used to say. An idiom now compromised by our understanding of triglycerides.

Remarriage, he noted, led to remodeling.

Remodeling: what precedes a wife's affair with the carpenter.

Apropos of Freud's thesis that a couple always has in the marital bed each mate's parents . . . . Throughout the waning years of his marriage, he often felt the presence of his wife's next husband.

My accountant's wife: after twenty years of marriage, she's left her husband and young daughter for — another woman. Years ago, this might have provoked controversy in my circle. Now, it barely raises a (pierced) eyebrow.

Not his fault: an autodidact, he had a bad teacher.

☙

After careful examination, his self-absorption was
found to result not from parental abuse but from a
kind of birth defect.

☙

"Gift of tongues." A soul en route to glossolalia but lingering at cunnilingus.

🙰

It was the curse of his weak constitution, his greatest health problem, that he could not abide hearing about the maladies of others.

Habitual — pre-emptive — self-reproach.

He'd grown afraid of winter.

His problem is that his soul looks like his body.

There came a point he realized he'd be changed not by traveling but by coming home.

A writer: someone willing to hurt others.

❧

Giacomo Leopardi, 19th century Italian poet, child genius, congenitally deformed, unlucky in love, and cursed with poor health. He wrote, "We have seen how very few people will be able to appreciate you when you succeed in becoming a perfect writer."

❧

Very positive fellow. Making an appointment with a therapist at his wife's urging, he learns he suffers from scoptophobia, that is, a fear of seeing what's right in front of his eyes.

Speaking as a failed vegetarian . . .

Paolo Uccello, the 15th century Florentine painter who established the rules of linear perspective. As Vasari wrote, "To pore over these things he remained in seclusion for months at a time," which apparently kept him impoverished. According to Uccello's wife, Uccello would work all night, and when she asked him to rest, he'd reply, "Oh, what a delightful thing is this perspective."

Afterword

I was forty-nine — me, once always the youngest, now going on fifty? — and *On Water* was soon to be published. I'd been saved by writing about water, by spending so much time in and on it the previous ten years. Doing so, having to do so, despite the risk that too much might be washed away. But then, suddenly, I was obsessed with — incessantly reading, and eager to learn the craft of, the import of — epigrams, aphorisms, apothegms. Nietzsche, Leopardi, Joubert, Chamfort, La Rochefoucauld, Lichtenberg, Porchia, Kraus, Jabès, Connolly, Martial, Pascal, Wilde, Chazal, Valéry, Cioran, Cunningham, Canetti. It might have been a cleansing of the writer's palate, but if I'd once been drawn to prose out of an impulse for the comprehensive, for narrative, now I wanted my stories very short, if stories at all.

Of course writing is a form of argument, an attempt to convince the reader that one character or another deserves sympathy, that this is how the world works, is the language of understanding. But as I got into the epigrammatic, I was interested most in the argument's conclusion. The story a given, or excluded except as backdrop. The form's very brevity an argument: why labor the obvious? As for the sentiments expressed . . . . Well, my mood was wintry, an insistence on the human capacity for self-deception in the service of self-interest.

And my language — oh, compressed, requiring attention, perhaps even a dictionary at hand.

But did I say argument? All this was peculiarly one-sided, left the reader little room for dialogue with the author, was almost pure assertion. Each short piece seemed to imply an unstated *quod erat demonstrandum*. Q.E.D.

Kronenberger, in his introduction to Merwin's translation of Chamfort, writes:

> English is a natural language for [the aphorism]. Unlike French, English can dispense with both the definite and indefinite article, can let the genitive ride on the nominative's back, and prepositions dance at sentences' ends; and can thus be more pointed, more concise, more splendidly lapidary.

And it is true, for the writer as craftsman there is an enormous delight in working this form. But content and tone are something else. Martial, in the first century A.D., and then La Rochefoucauld, in the seventeenth century, seem to have defined the form's air of disenchantment, the voice of the fallen or banished aristocrat. The men's hut, male writers in middle age. As Joseph Epstein writes, "The bone truth is that aphorisms, while they need not be bitter, are usually better for being so." And as La Bruyere argued, "No vice exists which does not pretend to be more or less like some virtue, and which does not take advantage of this assumed resemblance."

There was on the other hand the wistful Antonio Porchia, a real seeker: "Sometimes at night I light a

46

lamp so as not to see." Of Porchia's epigrams, Merwin wrote, "The distillate of suffering in some of the entries is pure and profound irony," but though I admired Porchia, he wasn't what I was after. Perhaps because, as Merwin observed, Porchia's was "an irony not of defense but of acceptance." No, I preferred, say, Lichtenberg, found overstatement well worth the risk: "A book is a mirror — when a monkey looks in, no apostle looks back out."

Martial and La Rochefoucauld. Playfully cruel. Acid. Scabrous: rough, harsh, somewhat indelicate. Passionate but detached, as if without illusions. Moralists moralizing. Punishing, implicating the reader with hard truths, forcing agreement. Self-absorbed, risking self-pity.

If the blues are an American idiom, in part because their formulaic laments are so confessional (Oprah Winfrey inevitably follows), epigrams are un-American. We believe in second chances, in mobility, insist we're a classless society. Our own most native epigrammatic impulse comes in the tag lines of Country and Western songs — "If the phone doesn't ring it's just me"; or "She got the gold mine, I got the shaft." Amiable, and clever, but, as with the Porchia, not what I was after.

The darker aspects of words. As revenge, for example: Swiftian, the adjective. Which means? Well, Swift's Gulliver, back home from his travels, unable to abide the stench of humans. Avoiding wife and children by staying out in the stable with the horses, who remind him of Houyhnhnmland's four-legged creatures of true reason. Misanthropy: hatred, distrust, of the species. (The triumph of honesty over hope, some say.)

47

Thackeray: "Ah, *Vanitas Vanitatum*! Which of us is happy in this world? Which of us has his desire? Or, having it, is satisfied? — Come, children, let us shut up the box and the puppets, for our play is played out."

As I worked in and around this form, I'd phone friends to convey what I was up to. They'd laugh, ruefully, think what they heard trenchant, tough. But later, several readers of the manuscript deemed my brevities, collectively, bleak, merciless, mean. Mean-spirited. Which left me disappointed, not in the news but in my friends. That is, I felt they were having trouble facing the truth. A bit late in the day, it seemed to me, for Pangloss, or to be getting squeamish.

Another friend, a very goodhearted poet (more positive a soul than I, but also old enough to know that one has to work at being goodhearted), observed that epigrams could lead right into silence. "At the end of that road is silence," is how she put it. And this, I had to admit, had merit. It wasn't simply that many of my compressions had to do with dying/death or foible/folly, but that they were, finally, a screed against language, against even bothering to continue the conversation. Which seemed to me at least one appropriate response to the world as I was experiencing it, like the behavior of the tribe that ceases to have children when its population falls below a certain level. Things were getting weird, no? When my sweet-souled poet friend, in any case, said that such epigrams could lead to silence, I responded, "There are worse things than silence."

If, however, I believed my epigrammatic writing had good cause, never did I not know that this was dabbling in a kind of black magic. (Not just the adolescent's bad behavior, or not even the coke freak's high, achieved with the understanding that the moment will be brief, the coming down rocky, the insights neon.)

Perhaps all art is black magic — Prospero's wand. No policemen in the heart and soul of the artist, as Conrad observed. Often, cackling madly after hammering out yet another line, I'd think of a friend in Southern California who'd become a compulsive writer of letters-to-the-editor. Long since, his brilliant calumnies had little to do with any effort to change minds.

About a year after I first noticed I'd become obsessed with the epigrammatic, I received a fellowship for a trip to Samoa: fallout from the water book. As I turned my attention to gathering materials for this return to the South Pacific, I noticed my addictive delight in the epigrammatic was beginning to moderate, though I did start culling what I'd come up with, preparing a short "final" manuscript. (A writer is someone who finishes things . . .) But the relentless need I'd had to write my compressions, as if they contained a mineral without which I could not survive, had abated. There is a tradition of eating dirt in both Africa and in the American South. Geophagy. Hungering for a certain taste or sustenance to the point of eating soil. ("The practice is found among peoples of low culture throughout the world," says the outdated *Webster's New International, Second Edition,* "and often develops an appetite or craving which favors idiocy . . . etc.") Not that I'd finished with the form — there was so much still to learn; I could spend years emulating Martial alone. Exposing myself to him, so to speak. Seeing what he brought out in me. But though I still wanted to pursue the craft of the epigrammatic, the sentiments the form seemed to induce in me no longer cried out to be expressed. And/or, I'd begun to tire of paradox, oxymoron, antithesis. Suddenly, inversions and apparent contradictions were too inevitable. Predictable, for all their surprises.

On my return from Samoa, when I once more made a decision to sit down at my desk, start that kind of travel — no passport needed — it was story, of all things, that was again an imperative. Everything and anything, past and present, what I could remember or reconstruct, what I knew or could imagine of the lives of others, all of it suddenly seemed both accessible and vital to speak of. I began writing at a ferocious pace. And after a month of early winter rain, there came a time when, heading out for my double cappuccino at dawn one November morning, I looked and saw a beautiful crescent cupping and illuminating the globe of the moon, fist of Jupiter pulsing just above. Saw, and wanted — oh, needed — to say so.

II

COMPRESSIONS: *A Second Helping*

"You do not know what life you live, or what you do, or who you are."

Dionysius in Euripides' *Bacchae*

"The bells of Hell go ting-a-ling-a-ling For you but not for me."

sung by WWI British troops

"I never lie," he says. Through his teeth, as it were.

⚬

"I never lie," he says. To others, he means.

⚬

Audible silence. The story of her life was she'd resolved not to tell it.

Zen of secrecy's eros: sound of one self-pleasuring.

Secrecy's promiscuity.

"You wasted your life," she says, flattering both herself and him.

"Beneath contempt." Down there somewhere.

Gratitude? Sing need, need.

Kissing cousins: opinion, hypocrisy.

Raised voices (should) raise skepticism.

Writer in study: house arrest.

♆

Not, of course, that he'd set out to become an un-published writer.

♆

That poem? Prose failing to go the distance.

What people don't see is how much work it was not to hold a job.

᠁

He claimed an emotional deduction for the cost of being rich.

᠁

Home Ec: on balance, cheaper to love than to hate.

❧

Their marriage worked until the market started to fall.

❧

She loves her husband, whom she deceives with a lover she deceives by letting him believe she loves him.

❦

Said the adulteress to her lover, "You're more interested in my marriage than I am."

❦

"My wife," he frequently says, even to those who know her proper name.

Her apparent hatred of her former husband was really just shame.

One of his palms cupping each breast. "I wish you had a third hand," she says.

She's lived with her boyfriend five years, never married because he doesn't want to, finally has an affair, is jilted by her lover. Seeing her so unhappy, the boyfriend proposes.

Wilt Chamberlain's "20,000" lovers. Yo, Wilt: Names?
Birthdays?

Know thyself: "Good thing I'm powerless," he muttered.

A Jew who veers Republican may need to have his foreskin examined.

Sweet sorrow: regret become rue.

❧

Remorse: biting one's own back.

❧

Suicide as an indirect indicator of strength: how long he'd been able to put up with himself.

"Don't speak ill of the dead." An enjoinder now attributed to J. Edgar Hoover.

⚡

"Don't speak ill of the dead." Next thing you know, they'll be telling us not to speak ill of the living!

⚡

"He deserved to die," she said. "He got off light."

Further Thoughts on the Epigrammatic

> Evolutionary psychology argues that exces-
> sive self-knowledge can be . . . a hindrance.
> If people perceive you as good and benevo-
> lent, they are more likely to accede to your
> desires. A good way to get others to believe
> that you are good and benevolent is to
> believe it yourself.
>
> — Oliver Morton

As readers of *The Price of the Ride* (1996) have
seen, the afterthoughts and repercussions of that short
book did not exhaust my interest in brevity, paradox,
or foible. Nor did these half-truths requite my desire
to encourage the reader to risk the distance from
premise to conclusion. As Jesse Green argues, the
reader must "work out, and usually backward, what
trajectory led from takeoff to landfall . . . ." Though
Green believes such a task is created with "more than
a hint of sadism," I confess only to be asserting that
this is the world we live in, the tongue of understanding. Using the enchantment of language to express . .
. oh, aspects of disenchantment, brief briefs about or
against what we profess to hold to be true.

Given my experience in this form, what words come to mind to further describe its component energies? Well . . .

TEMPTATION. "I have written a wicked book," Melville wrote Hawthorne about *Moby Dick*, "and feel spotless as the lamb." Surely, stripping away narrative in favor of conclusion, the epigrammist savors the risk of being wrongheaded/reductionist/unfair.

RETALIATION (though the form may appear to possess a first strike capability). The proverbial revenge against reality. And, always, what one would like to have said. *Avoir un esprit de l'escalier*: one's belated repartee — *quand il n'est plus temps, qui se manifeste en retard* — as, out the door, one heads down the staircase. "I as much as told him," a friend of mine said, recounting an argument he was winning in the retelling.

BONSAI. A mix of envisioning, pruning, shaping, caring. Stunting. Making something perfect, if on a diminished scale. Improving (?) nature. Delight in doing something harder than it looks.

POINTILLISM. Going after the luminous by small discrete increments, dots of color the hues of which are to be mixed, recomposed, made into shapes by the reader's eye.

As for the views of others about such endeavor, after reading *The Price of the Ride* a friend claimed a line as his own creation. Maybe he'd heard me tell it to him before? Nope. Whatever: not my favorite, I explained. Someone else felt a fragment was about him. I did what I could — "It's an if-the-shoe-fits type of deal," I said.

And a poet I know observed that epigrams are "poems without wings." This good writer momentarily perhaps not "afraid enough of poetry," as George Open once put it.

Another correspondent suggested the little book as a whole made a kind of ghazal? Zhazam! An ancient form, it turns out — short lyrics, couplets intensely compressed — from Persian literature, appearing later in Urdu poetry, part of the Islamic legacy. But my work a ghazal? Go figure.

Ghazal or no, I had been obsessed with compression. Even early on in my prose experience, what to leave out of a story compelled as much as what to put in. I thought mastery more possible within a small frame, an odd notion, perhaps. By the time *Who Wrote the Book of Love?* (1977) was published, I'd been working in prose units no longer than several pages, some of these fables of contemporary life only half a page, none with titles, characters often unnamed.

By *Compared to What?* (1988), my third-person non-fiction meditation on writing and the writer's life, I felt free to have "chapters" one or two lines long. I liked the white space, saw no reason poets should have sole possession of such rich terrain. A "Take Back the Night" situation, as far as I was concerned. Poet/translator Stephen Mitchell, reading an early draft of *The Price of the Ride*, suggested that setting the brevities one or two to a page would test their strength. Right he was, but I also enjoyed the sensation that so much blank page was illicit. (Edmond Jabs believed that white space "is much stronger and more violent than the text . . . It's necessary that writing have a great space in and of itself to support the white space.")

The epigrammatic, Jesse Green writes, "Where pornography is rape, wit must be, too, for wit is intellectual pornography, stimulating for the sake of stimulation . . ." Here I demur, and not only because pornography is not rape, whatever the delight of so erroneous a comparison. Really, wit's just another kind of pleasure, but, in the epigrammatic, didactic: hard truths are broached, cases made. If we are to consider the epigrammatic and sex, perhaps the link is to (fore) play, however penetrating the insight.

Finally, inevitably, the question of misanthropy. Are these premortems, these mordents, tarts & tales, bad for the spirit? No medicinal value — diuretic, if not cathartic? Surely it's worth something to articulate such complexities as the music of language allows. Then too, there's the joy of trying to achieve the verbal equivalent of a prime number. Of working one's way toward the irreducible (and so un-translatable). Forget even the theoretical possibility of paraphrase! What was said, is. And though bitterness may be the risk of satire, we may conclude that love of even the weapon is, nonetheless, a form of love.

To know more than one can say. Or so say I. Told you so. Tell you what. You know what I mean.

III

TONGUE-TIED:

A Breviary of Cautions & Savors

Breviary: a book of daily prayers, from Latin, *breviarium, abridgement.*

It's hard to be human and hide the wet spot.

— Dr. William Santis

Q: Have I wasted my whole life?

A: No. Not yet.

Spring makes light of winter's sorrows.

꙰

He wouldn't recognize the truth if it walked past him naked.

Surprising, not that he lived alone, but that he could live with himself.

<p>

Alone. Why people get cats, dogs. Married.

<p>

Spacious bedroom. Room for misunderstanding.

❧

Not a turn-on: she'd never been spanked as a child.

❧

She hopes he doesn't fuck like he eats.

Right, humor's aggressive component. But then, difference between a joke and a war?

🙶

He tells her, "You're my soul." Which he fails to save.

Yo, jilted lovers! Don't argue with the dead when they're still alive.

He died not of heartbreak but from a case of severely strained credulity.

His adultery? The high-minded kind.

Devoted to both wife and lover. Loyal to a fault.

Calmly stating the obvious, the Zen acolyte notes that Jesus's violent demise shows He had "unfinished business." An argument perhaps best resolved when the acolyte is on his own deathbed. Or cross.

※

Q. Since nothing happens without a higher purpose, what was the higher purpose when the spiritual seeker left his wife?

A: To be with another woman.

※

Writer. Blocked? Or, nothing (he's willing) to confess.

※

Writer's block? Like everyone, writers block out quite a bit.

※

Charity to a friend, then melancholy. Dismay at the friend's fate? Self-pity?

Writer, home from a fellowship abroad, informs listeners that travel broadens. William Blake, Emily Dickinson, and Henry David Thoreau having, so to speak, missed the boat.

❧

"Being famous is hard," the writer confides, startling the interviewer, who'd understood her to be momentarily newsworthy.

❧

Selfish writer. Philanthropist of the arts?

❧

Passion's nomenclature. "Whore": what her lover called her for fucking her husband.

॰

Still with her husband-the-jogger? Cuckolds have legs!

॰

Afraid. Of, for instance, being alone with a book.

⚡

Quiet. Worth a great deal.
Too quiet. Worth even less.

⚡

Capable of doing without, her sacrifices were mostly human.

꙰

The atomic half-life of self-deprecation. Persistently briefer than the need to deprecate others.

꙰

Penis. Clinical, like vulva, most frequently qualified only by the possessive, i.e., his penis. Prick, on the other hand, like cunt, can take another adjective or two.

&

Concluding she seemed virginal but wasn't, he resolved to privilege not adjectives but nouns.

&

"Still in love?" the husband offers by way of salutation, before one can ask after his wife the heiress.

ॐ

"You're larger than life," they tell him.

That is:

1. they fear they're not really living, and
2. they're glad not to be larger than life.

Viagra'd penis: friend standing up for you.

Viagra'd penis: mind of its own.

Viagra joke? Penis as stand-up comedian.

Viagra: makes your member remember.

Rap Viagra: got yo' back? Naw, yo' front.

❧

Use of the word small for one's partner's penis? Self-fulfilling and self-denying.

❧

Fans at ball games screaming obscenities. A kind of Halloween, but is it masks on or masks off?

✗

Idiomatic American English. Not very easy: "Please." Surprisingly difficult: "You're welcome."

✗

Jealousy:

equals self-knowledge;

indicted for hyperbole, guilty of understatement;

demanding proof of what never happened.

Re: free translation . . . Preposterous, from the Latin.
Ass backwards.

You haven't really lived till you don't want to live anymore.

⚥

"As good as dead." And gettin' better all the time.

⚥

Obituaries. Death notices. Death notices? Sure: Death doesn't miss a (living) thing.

ॐ

Winter darkness. The end is nigh(t).

ॐ

Epitaph:
SEE YOU SOON

⚘

Last line of our tale?
Death sentence.

⚘

Testaments & Mea Culpas

Recently, I turned sixty. Sixty — a wonder-working number as thirty, forty, fifty never were. Over the years, I'd experienced a bemused remove from the dismay of others confronting such benchmarks. But sixty? I felt . . . fast-forwarded. Victim of mistaken identity. Read the digits as a measure of my debt to time, like a losing gambler at evening's end who'd almost convinced himself the chips were . . . just chips.

More, I was faintly embarrassed, as if having contracted a social disease. Sixty? Not that there wasn't fair warning. As I turned fifty-four, an artery in my heart tried to "occlude." Close call, but life went on. Then, two years ago, I became the friend of a woman in her mid-thirties who worked with "seniors," the "over-sixties." Of course I realized I'd soon qualify to be one of her clients. Picking her up at work, I couldn't fail to see wheelchairs in the lobby. Wheelchairs are for others? Also, receiving still another fifth-year report from my college class, I was sobered by the growing number of death notices. *Memento mori*: Remember that thou must die. I'd presumed an exemption. Son of a famous physician who built the world's first hospital for the care of children with cancer — about a mile from our beautiful home — I grew up with the capacity to make an absolute distinction between those dying kids and my

111

siblings and self. Years later, arriving in California at twenty, I had the sensation there was no dying here, so much milder the climate, so much freer of the dead hand of the past than my native Boston.

Just sixty, then, and though sixty's the former fifty, I reread "The Snow Man," Wallace Stevens arguing you need "a mind of winter" to behold "the boughs/ Of the pine-trees crusted with snow." A mind of winter: this time, the phrase spoke both of one's response to the physical world and to my animus for a third batch of (very brief) winter's tales.

See the dying man? "Not long for this world," they say, albeit (albeit!) less than they used to. "Not long for this world." Passing out of usage. Archaic because of the hint of euphemism, suggestion of something to come? When, recently, I heard the phrase uttered by a vital eighty-four year old doctor/surfer in Honolulu, the words entered my ears as imperative: you should not long for this world. Though of course we do, we do.

Composing oneself. The last four decades (ha! there is an erotics of being able to invoke so much [mis] spent time) . . . I say, the last four decades I've been impelled to write from a not unusual mix of motives. Emulating books I admired; sense of author as hero, magician; exhilaration of supplicating, dancing with language. Hunger to set straight, restore. Not to mention words like vainglory, memorialize, lament. But as the writer ages, whatever his habitual mode or fluency, though the number of letters in the alphabet remains constant, stories written and unwritten seem to undergo transformation. At the least, by a certain age the author surely better knows of what he speaks. Can sometimes more freely acknowledge self-interest, self-deception. Concede the limits of art: how much can it redeem; for whom redemptive?

Alternatively, p.o.v. of the text, perhaps stories increasingly manifest their own agenda. "Yo, this is your story speaking." Might the stories be compared to:

1. teenage males, voices cracking, tremulously insisting on their own (passionately contrary) narrative of what you thought you'd been living with them?

2. caged lions that, after years of compliance, maul the tamer?

3. a terrorist sleeper cell biding its time?

Or perhaps there are different storytelling centers within each of us. Imagine Freud's imaginary Ego, Superego, and Id each having its own narrative. Imagine three or five other aspects of the self! Perhaps all their stories are always being told, like radio stations sending out signals at the same time, but, as years pass the writer has less strength to insist on "his" version. To resist the stories' version? For the male writer, it may coincide with the waning of testosterone haze, occasioning a new — pristine; bewildering — ability, willingness, to see. Or perhaps stories never do not know they're only stories, and — approaching our end, which is to say, their host's demise — note that our blood is thinning, are not reluctant to let on.

But, really, how plumb the motives of stories? Perhaps, instead, we should think in terms of the visual — a mere change of perspective. For years, it's all mostly before you; room for improvement, correction. The triumph of Your Real Story can still take place, to which the past is subordinated. But what's behind you accumulates; space for new narrative foreshortens, unless you're extending your saga into The Life to Come (which has its own hazards — Hell, for instance).

There may even be some concommitant enlightenment. Think of the heroic polar explorer stranded on the ice floe who, eating his shoe, finally acknowledges no rescue's forthcoming. A coming to terms perhaps influenced by the sight of shoe-eating colleagues. No rescue. Why, then, do some (most?) writers persist in their earlier narratives? Oh, adult life as nursery school, cont'd: one more gold star on the forehead. Why be reckless in service of the truth, what if you can beat the game, if there's no reckoning? What if the disguise still works, or truth's just too painful — for writer, audience. Lear terrifies, but, leaving the theatre, we reestablish distance: foolish Lear, and a king to boot! Not like us, and we have no heaths over here anyway.

But those gold stars on the forehead. Think of poets playing the poet. What if each oracular *pronunciamento* takes one further from what he might have been able to say? "Poetry as Breath," for instance. (Oh, jeez, kiss my breath.) So many self-serving fairytales about our lives, told by writers.

Q: So, T.F., your "cautions and savors" tell the whole truth?

A: Nope. Sorry. Epigrams are, well, polished shards. Karl Kraus said, "an aphorism never coincides with the truth," is "either a half-truth or a one-and-a-half-truth."

Whether or not that is true, epigrams may be breadcrumbs marking the writer's path home to . . . silence, or to more extended prose. Or may function as prods, reminding the word-worker about word joy. Or implicate and so chasten, once more evoking the personal the writer projected as universal (what Kafka called transforming I-madness into he-madness).

For the American writer, another appeal of the epigrammatic is its (near) (utter) unmarketability. What is the relationship of writer and audience? Disdain (dis+deign)? Perhaps too strong a word (and often paired with craven need), but how little response should one hope for? Years ago, working as a consultant at a foundation-funded conference, well-paying labor in a good cause, I sat in a hotel banquet room suffering through interminable first-day Power-Pointed remarks. Sand rivering down, down through the waist of life's hourglass. Looking over at my colleague's laptop as he typed frenetically — conference journaling, I thought; hard-working to a fault — I realized my colleague was completing an overdue report for another foundation. Our eyes met. "Fuck 'em if they can't take a joke," he said. Kept typing. Though, soon after the conference, my colleague died quite prematurely — alcohol; cigarettes; angry wit — I now, as epigrammist, often think of his admonition.

But my manuscript. Only lately, *Tongue-Tied* was still awaiting "completion." I'd been working at it four years, now and then coming up with another one-liner. Revising the accumulation yet again, trying to get at core verbal impulse. For several months, however, I'd done little "real" writing. Mostly teaching, salsa danc-ing, a commissioned film treatment, e-mail. I liked be-ing in the "pure present tense," as I have construed it, how I imagine most people live, though I did miss the closure of my study, the routine of solo labor, all that order to keep. Not really writing, in any case, I'd reached the point where I could no longer tell whether I was doing myself a favor or inflicting deprivation. Avoiding or inducing megalomania.

Meanwhile, in Hawaii — surfing, more salsa — I set myself the task of rereading my recent novel, *The Beholder* (2001). Took four weeks to get through it, as-sessing words, sentences, structure of scenes, remem-bering what was left out, reworked how through so many drafts. The DVD of my novel! Was, in the end, moved, admiring. Not self-congratulatory: another self wrote it, in another life-time — five years earlier for the first draft, and that initial applied dreaming built on years of reading and research (!) about pornography and repre-sentations of the nude female form. (Around the time I'd turned sixty, an old friend came across *The Beholder*, called to say she loved it. "You must have women lined up at the front door waiting to seduce the author." I put down the phone, went to check.)

So: back from Hawaii, I began to edit the interview Melville scholar Sam Otter had conducted with me about my Pacific writings, in particular my many references to Moby Dick. At one point I'd said to Sam, "There I was in the Pacific. I needed it. I had the great feeling almost nobody else was writing about this world with candor, much less with skill . . . . I felt I owned it." Reading these lines, I was suddenly impelled to again think of myself as a writer, as if I'd just remembered a terribly important appointment at the last possible moment. An "Ah, of course" sort of deal. And at this moment, what kind of writer would I be? There by my desk was the folder of unpublished epigrams, one to a page, pulsing on the shelf like my computer's green light in "Sleep" mode. I'd been letting them . . . mature, stew, metastasize. Manifest their weaknesses. In that instant of recovery of the writerly self (or of once more displacing some better self), I was again an epigrammist, member of a small, strange cohort, but once more entitled to its malices, savors, apercus, ripostes, errors. At this moment, the labor was hands-on, shaping, smoothing, wordsmith as bikini wax specialist crafting the perfect Brazilian cut. "Far out," as they used to say in the days I had long hair. I was, happily, back at work.

And in my orbit, as always, other artists at work. Young Michael, teaching himself to be a writer, reading my books carefully, gleaning. Very talented Laura, year five on her novel. Leo, eighty, with the manuscript of a masterful new story collection. Chester, past eighty, still centering his passionate life around the freedom to write, publishing one new book, another. And in my orbit, as always, artists not at work: H—, for instance, who has the latest computer and ergonomic chair but is unable to sit still at his desk. Where did that capacity go? Perhaps for too long he didn't risk enough, in the end forgot how. Committing to words is a tough game.

Committing to words. Joyce Carol Oates, in *The Faith of a Writer*, argues: "To write is to invite angry censure . . . . Art by its nature is a transgressive act, and artists must accept being punished for it. The more original and unsettling their art, the more devastating their punishment."

Q: Tom, what do you think of that quote?

T. F.: Must I answer?

Q: Please.

T. F.: Well . . . yes, no. Sometimes. Actually, the more common curse of art is that you may not be sure you deserve praise. Or, one's own judgments may be the most severe. Lately, for instance, I've been subjected to a nightly pre-dawn barrage of berating, and not from others. Surely this too will pass. In addition, I've found myself easily moved to tears. Just the kind of thing my mother would have deplored. And bad for the epigrammist? Well, there's Frost's line, "No tears in the writer, no tears in the reader." But I also think of my friends in Boston so many, many years ago, how among ourselves we ten-year-olds talked tough and surly. Eat it raw; old enough to bleed/old enough to butcher; up yours; no shit Dick Tracy. Add a few other lines, and you'd achieve fluency in our lingua franca. But we also well knew what it was to be "crying mad," turned away at the sight of tears in others. For the grown-up epigrammist, then, perhaps the motto should be, "No flinching." Something we kids used to say, in moments long ago long lost, when it was again our turn to strike the blow.

© David Lance Goines

Recipient of Guggenheim, National Endowment, Rockefeller, Fulbright, and Dorothea Lange-Paul Taylor fellowships, author of many works of fiction and creative nonfiction, Thomas Farber is Senior Lecturer in English at the University of California, Berkeley. Visit *thomasfarber.org*

Other books from Hip Pocket Press:

New California Voices Series

YOU NOTICE THE BODY, Gail Rudd Entrekin, 1998

TERRAIN, Dan Bellm, Molly Fisk & Forrest Hamer, 1999

A COMMON ANCESTOR, Marilee Richards, 2000

Anthology

SIERRA SONGS & DESCANTS: POETRY & PROSE OF THE SIERRA, 2002

HPP
HIP POCKET PRESS

HIP POCKET PRESS
228 Commercial St. Box 138
Nevada City, CA 95959
Book Orders: www.hippocketpress.com

www.ingramcontent.com/pod-product-compliance
Lightning Source LLC
Chambersburg PA
CBHW031322040426
42443CB00005B/187